SPARK WITHOUT FIRE OF 2 CHAPS

CHAPTER - 2

GYAN CHAND PATTANAYAK

Made with ♥ on the Notion Press Platform
www.notionpress.com

EYE WOULD LIKE TO DEDICATE THIS CHAPTER -2 TO ALL THE READERS AND FOLLOWERS OF CHAPTER -1 BECAUSE THE POETIC JOURNEY IS ALL ABOUT HEALTHY UNDERSTANDING OF THE NOUNS AND PRONOUNS ALONG WITH VERBS WHICH IS ALWAYS IN - TRASITIVE MODE AND ALSO EYE DEDICATE THIS CHAPTER -2 TO THE READERS WHO BELIEVE ON THE SUBJECT LIGHTS WHICH TRAVELS FASTER THAN SOUND TO AWAKEN EYES.......

EYE DON'T HAVE CAPTION FOR THIS SPARK WITHOUT FIRE

Contents

Foreword *ix*

Preface *xi*

Acknowledgements *xiii*

Prologue *xv*

SPARK WITHOUT FIRE CHAPTER - 2

SPARK WITHOUT FIRE

SPARK WITHOUT FIRE

SPARK WITHOUT FIRE

SPARK WITHOUT FIRE

SPARK WITHOUT FIRE

SPARK WITHOUT FIRE

SPARK WITHOUT FIRE

SPARK WITHOUT FIRE

SPARK WITHOUT FIRE

SPARK WITHOUT FIRE

Spark Without Fire 25

Spark Without Fire 27

Spark Without Fire 29

Foreword

TOUR FROM INFINITY FOR A REASON
IN FLUCTUATE SEASON
WITH THE HELP AVIATION
TO CREATE A NEW VISION
THIS IS THE FOREHEAD FOR ALL TIME AND FOR
ALL UPCOMING CHAPTERS OF
"SPARK WITHOUT FIRE"
A POETIC JOURNEY WITH THIS
ALLITERATION.........

Preface

A POETIC JOURNEY OF ZERO WHO CREATE AN UNIQUE NUMERIC VALUES WITH THE HELP OF LIGHT AND ALSO A JOURNEY OF A MALE AND A FEMALE IN A ZERO - ONE NUMERIC VERSION. EYE AM IN A FRAME OF ZERO TO CIRCUMNAVIGATE THOUGHTS FOR THE ADORABLE ONE ..

Acknowledgements

EYE ALWAYS BELIEVE IN THE LIGHTS BECAUSE LIGHT HAS THE ONLY AND SUPREME POWER TO CREATE ZERO.

Prologue

THE POETIC JOURNEY WITH LIGHT IS ABOUT TO PRESERVE THE TREASURE AND EYE TRUST LIGHT BECAUSE LIGHT HAS A BIG CONTAINER WHICH CONTAINS THE PAST PRESENT AND ALSO FUTURE ITINERARIES...

SPARK WITHOUT FIRE

CHAPTER - 2

TOUR FROM INFINITY FOR A REASON

IN FLUCTUATE SEASON

WITH THE HELP OF AVIATION

TO CREATE A NEW VISION

EYE LOVE EARTH BECUASE IT HAS ALWAYS A CHPATER OF ZERO FOR THE ONE ADORATION BECAUSE THIS THEORY OF LOVE SAYS ZERO COULD BE ONE IN A SQUARE LIGHT COMBINATION. WHEN EVALUATE THE EYE LIFE OF ZERO THEN ONE THING EYE FIGURED OUT ABOUT ZERO IS THAT A ZERO WAS BORN WITH THE PRESENT TIME AND FOR THE ONE IT STARTED REPRESENT THE PAST WITH PRESENT CONTINUING LIFE AND THE MOST INTERESTING FACT THAT THE ZERO HAS FUTURE TIME EXHIBITION

WHEN EYE AM TALKING ABOUT ZERO THEORY THEN EYE AM FORSURE ABOUT THE CONSEQUENCES OF LIGHT PERHAPS LIGHT IS ONLY WITENESSED NOUN OF PAST ,PRESENT AND FUTURE ZERO LIFE AND

LIGHT NEVER ARGUE WITH SOUND FOR THE CALENDER DEPICTION .

A NEVER ENDING CHPATER OF A LIGHT WHEN MINGLE WITH A F-LIGHT ,IT CREATE A SPARK OF DELIGHT WHICH HAS THEIR OWN WAY OF A CANDLITE AND EYE AS A ZERO COULD BE FLAUNT BY THE ONE IN REAL FRONT REAR MIRROR NAVIGATION.

EYE WAS BORN AS ZERO AND OPENED EYES WITH THE ONE WHO HAS CARRIED FOR SEVERAL MONTH AND THE FIRST SNAP WHICH EYE CAPTURED THROUGH THE LIGHT WAS AN OLD VERSION ALONG WITH THE PRESENT TIME OF THIS WONDER PEREGRINATION

SPARK WITHOUT FIRE

TOUR FROM INFINITY FOR A REASON

IN FLUCTUATE SEASON

WITH THE HELP OF AVIATION

TO CREATE A NEW VISION

LIFE IS ALWAYS BLESSED BE HAVING THE NATURAL LIGHT AND LIGHT WITH THE EYE BALL WHICH HAS NATURAL SIGN OF ZERO BUT THIS ZERO CAN VIEWED THE LONGEST DISTANCE AS LONG AS IT CAN VIEWED IN A HORIZONTAL DIRECTION OF EVERY ANGLE AND CAN TRAVERSE THROUGH BILLIONS OF MILE IN VERTICAL DIRECTION OF ALL ANGLE WITH THE JOURNEY OF RENTED LIGHT YEARS COLLABORATION.

RE-DICOVER OF ZERO IN THE BREATHING INHABITATION SOMETIMES HARD AND IMMPOSIBLE IN TERMS OF THIS POSITIVE AND NEGATIVE INTEGERS BECAUSE AS EYE TOLD EARLIER SENTENCES ABOUT HOW THE LIGHT HAS BEEN CARRIED FOR SEVERAL MONTHS IN A CRITICAL PATHWAYS FOR ILLUMINATION..

WHEN EYE WAS BORN , EYE WAS LOOKING FOR THE ONE WHO CAN EVALUATE THE VALUE AND CELEBRATE ALL MAGICAL; MOMENTS BEING ONE ATTIRE FABRICATION AND IN SEARCH OF THAT ONE SOMETIMES EYE HAS TO RESIDE AND TO CLICK MORE AND MORE OLD AS WELL AS MORE OLDER SNAPS WTH ITS PRESENT OCCUPATION AND THE NUMBER OF EYES TO WHOM EYE HAVE ALREADY INTERACTED FOR THE ADORABLE ONE, PERHAPS FOR THE FUTURE MANIFESTATION..

SPARK WITHOUT FIRE

TOUR FROM INFINITY FOR A REASON

IN FLUCTUATE SEASON

WITH THE HELP OF AVIATION

TO CREATE A NEW VISION

AS EYE KNOW AND ASSIMILATED WITH THE FACT THAT A RENTED LIGHT YEARS JOURNEY NEVER BE A PERMANENT SOLUTION OF ANY ARITHMETIC VERSION BECAUSE THE EYE BALL LIGHT WHO HAS FIRST STARTED SEEING THE ALL MOST COUNTABLE BREATHING ORGANS BUT STILL TO REWIRE ITS SENSE FOR THE ONE IN THE JOURNEY OF HEATHY FASTER LIGHT COMMUNICATION ..

THE HARDEST FACT ABOUTTHE ZERO SIGN EYE BALL THAT IT CAN NOT CHANGE THE FACT WHAT IT SEES THROUGH THE LIGHT BECAUSE THE MOMENTS CAPTURED BY BLINKS OF EYES TRUELY CONNECTED TO SAFEST AND LOCKED MEMORY BOX AND THE UNIQUE ONE IS ONLY KEY WHICH HAS THE ALL TYPE OF SIMILARITIES TO UNLOCK THE MEMORY BOX ,EITHER FOR CONTRUCTION OR FOR DESTRUCTION.

EYE WAS THINKING ABOUT THE ZERO'S ONE JOURNEY ON THE CIRCLE OF DARK BUT WITH LOADS OF HOPE AND COURAGE AND EYE SCREAMED THROUGH THE DARK TUNNEL BECAUSE HERE IS A BELIEVE THAT THERE IS ALWYAS LIGHT OF AT THE END OF TUNNELFOR THE ONE WHO CONTINUOSLY WORKING FOR THE DESTINATION IN A RENTED LIGHT YEARS TOUR OF LIFE FOR SCINTILLATION.

SPARK WITHOUT FIRE

TOUR FROM INFINITY FOR A REASON

IN FLUCTUATE SEASON

WITH THE HELP OF AVIATION

TO CREATE A NEW VISION

WHEN EYE TRIED TO DISTINGUISH BETWEEN THE NATURAL LIGHT YEARS AND THE RENTED LIGHT YEARS THEN EYE FOUND A HUGE SCARY FACT ABOUT BOTH LIGHT YEARS BECAUSE TODAYS DIGITAL WORLD EYE CONNECTED EVEN 15,OOO MILES BY DIALING FEW DIGITS ON A DEVICE WHICH MOBILIZE EVERY WORDS AS WELL AS TRANSPORTED EYE WORDS WITHIN FEW FRACTION OF SECONDS BUT EYE STILL DIDN'T UNDERSTAND ABOUT THIS JOURNEY OF MORE THAN THOUSANDS OF DIFFERENT LANGUAGE IN A SINGLE PLATFORM FOR EYE LIGHT ASSCENTUATION ..

THE NATURAL LIGHT WHICH TRAVERSE THROUGH FROM INFINITY FOR A REASON HAS ALWAYS DEVELOPED A SIGN OF NATURAL GROWTH EDITION BUT THE RENTED LIGHT YEARS HAS AN EDITED

JOURNEY OF NATURAL LIGHT FOR TRANSFORMATION AND THE ZERO WHO LONGING FOR THE ONE IS A BLEND OF NATURAL AS WELL AS RENTED LIGHT YEARS VERSION .

ONE ZERO EYE WAS THINKING ABOUT THE ONE WHO WILL ACCOMPLISH THE TOUR AND SET A VALUE FOR ZERO ,SO ZERO EYE HAS STARTED FINDING THE ROUTES TO REACH THE ONE IN THE CIRCLE OF DARK AND USED TO NOTICE THE NATURAL LIGHT EVERYDAY AND ASKED FOR THE WAY TO FIND OUT THAT ONE TO MERGE WITH ZERO FOR A VALUE ADDITION ..

SPARK WITHOUT FIRE

TOUR FROM INFINITY FOR A REASON

IN FLUCTUATE SEASON

WITH THE HELP OF AVIATION

TO CREATE A NEW VISION

EYE WAS THINKING ABOUT THE NATURAL LIGHT SOURCE WHICH TRAVELS THROUGH THE SQUARE TO SHED LIGHT ON ZERO'S FUNCTION AND THE ZERO WHO HAS BUBBLE OVER WITH IDEAS TO FIND OUT THE ONE FOR AN ADMIRATION AND THE JOURNEY OF ZERO WAS NOT THAT AS EASY AS IT LOOKS LIKE OF A MIRROR CONFRONTATION ,

AS AN AUTHOR EYE HEARD ABOUT ZERO - ONE BINARY SYSTEM IN DIGITALIZATION WHERE CODES HAVE BEEN SHARED FOR SAFETY TAKE OFF AS WELL AS LANDING IN EVERY DIGITAL FORMAT ALSO IN A HOLE SHAPE ONE AVIATION , SO ZERO HAS ADOPTED THE PAST PUBLISHED THEORIES LIKE THE PYRAMID HIERARCHIAL THEORY IN A DARK CIRCLE ,LINEAR THEORY AND THE SQUARE THEORY TO UNDERSTAND AS WELL AS FIGURED OUT THE ANGLE

ONE ,

ZERO WAS FULLY AWARE ABOUT THE FACT THAT RENTED LIGHT YEARS LIFE HAS ALMOST STARTED WANDERING INSIDE THE DARK CIRCLE FOR THE ANGLE ONE WHO WOULD BE VERY HAPPY BY HAVING THE ZERO FOR MORE VALUE CREATION BUT DROOL OVER THE ONE ANGLE IN A TRIANGLE WHICH LOOKS LIKE THE SHAPE OF A PYRAMID WAS VERY HARD AND ALSO AN UNACCEPTABLE ROUTE BECAUSE HERE ZERO HAS TO STEP INTO AN EXTINGUISHED LIGHT SUBJECT IN ITS WAY OF FOREHEAD EMOTION ...

SPARK WITHOUT FIRE

TOUR FROM INFINITY FOR A REASON

IN FLUCTUATE SEASON

WITH THE HELP OF AVIATION

TO CREATE ANEW VISION

AS AN AUTHOR IT WAS VERY DIFFICULT FOR ME TO NARRATE THE ZERO'S JOURNEY FOR THE ONE IN AN EXTRAORDINARY PLATFORM WHERE MANY KINDS OF JOKES ,MEMES SPROUTED UP IN VARIOUS TRIANGLE BECAUSE WHEN ROBOT HAS STARTED ASKING USER THAT ARE YOU A ROBOT ? AND THE USER HAS A CLEAR REPLY TO THE DISGITAL MACHINE WITH TICKING THE BOX AS A HUMAN SUBSTANTIATION ,

THEN EYE COULD THINK ABOUT HOW THE ZERO DID GET THE ONE FOR AND WHERE DID THE ZERO GET THE ONE IN THIS JOURNEY LIMITED LIGHT YEARS MANIFESTATION AND AS AN AUTHOR EYE FORSURE ABOUT TRUTH OF ASTROID STARS WHICH HAS AN EXISTENCE FOR BOTH PURPOSE OF JUVENATION ,

AND EYE AS AN AUTHOR THE JOURNEY OF ZERO WAS NOT THAT EASY AS ONE CAN IMAGINE IN A TRIANGLE ROUTE IN A DARK CIRCLE ,OK NOW ZERO SET FORTH FOR THE CRAZY ONE AND THIS TRIANGL;E ROUTE FIRST ZERO STARTED RESEARCHING SOME ONE WHO PROBABLY WOULD HAVE BEEN PROMOTING THE TRIANGLE ROUTE AND GUIDE SPECIES IN TO THEIR LOVEABLE DESTINATION ..

SPARK WITHOUT FIRE

TOUR FROM INFINITY FOR A REASON

IN FLUCTUATE SEASON

WITH THE HELP OF AVIATION

TO CREATE A NEW VISION

FINALLY THE SEARCH OF EXPONENT CAME TO AN END WHEN MET WITH EX AND EX HAS A VERY SOUND KNOWLEDGE ON TRIANGLE ROUTE , WELL EYE AM NOT TALKING ABOUT " BARMUDA TRIANGLE " BECAUSE ACCORDING TO DISTINCTIVE THEORIES THIS WAS A KIND OF THEORY IF SOMEONE HAS A REGULAR PRACTICE IN THIS ROUTE THEN ITS VERY EASY TO GET THE ONE IN THIS BLUR DARK CIRCLE AREA LIMITATION AND THE TRIANGLE ROUTE WAS FAMOUS ROUTE METHOD FERRETED OUT ANYTHING IN AN INNER DARK CIRCLE SUB-STATION,

NOW ZERO WAS PART OF THE GUIDED TOUR WHICH LEAD BY EX AND ZERO HAD FULL FLEDGED CONFIDENCE ON EX BECAUSE THE MOMENT ZERO STARTED INTERACTING WITH EX, REALISED THE POWER OF EX 'S EXPONENT AND WAS QUITE HAPPY

BECAUSE THE DREAMS TO GET THE ONE HAS ALREADY FALLED IN THE SAFE HAND OF PWER MULTIPLING EXPONENT AND ZERO WAS QUITE EXCITED IN THIS VULNERABLE TRIANGLE TRANSITION ,

WITH THE YEARS OF TRANSITION WITH THE POWER EXPONENT EX IN THIS EXPONENTIAL EQUATION TOUR HAD CREATED MANY NUMBER OF SAME PAGES AND MANY NUMBER OF SAME LINES BUT STILL THE ONE TO WHOM ZERO LOOKING FOR WAS FARAWAY FROM THE LIGHT VISION ....

SPARK WITHOUT FIRE

TOUR FROM INFINTY FOR A REASON

IN FLUCTUATE SEASON

WITH THE HELP OF AVIATION

TO CREATE A NEW VISION

EVEN THE EX WANTED TO KNOW THE REASON
BEHIND THIS CURIOSITY OF ZERO FOR THE ONE
AND IN THS SAME PAGES, IN SAME LINES EX ASKED
ZERO WHY ARE YOU SO HASTY FOR THE ONE ONLY
WHEN MAXIMUM OPTIONS ARE LINED UP IN THIS
TRIANGLE FENESTRATION ,

BUT ZERO HAD NO ANSWER FOR THIS RIDICULOUS QUESTION OF EX , EXCEPT A FUGITIVE SMILE , THEN EX UNDERSTOOD THE MEANING OF THIS FUGITIVE SMILE AND STRETCHED OUT THE HAND FOR COOPERATION AND STARTED DELIVERING THE TRIANGLE ROUTE WHERE BOTH HAVE TO FORGED THROUGH DARK CIRCLE EVEN AT BACKNECK SPEED ,IN THEIR INITIAL JOURNEY EX WAS EXPLAINGING THE ROUTING POINTS ONE BY ONE FOR A SMOOTH MOVEMENT WITHOUT ANY TERMS AND CONDITION

,

THOUGH EX HAD SOUND KNOWLEGE ABOUT THE ROUTING IN TRIANGLE ,AS A ROUTER EX TAUGHT ZERO ,WE NEED TO BE MORE CONSCIOUS IN THIS ROUTE BECAUSE HAD TO ENCOUNTERED WITH STROMS LIKE A NEW BORN CHILD LEARNED TO WALK BUT SUDDENLY FOUND ITS FEETS THROUGH THE RUNNING WHEEL DUE TO UNCONSCIOUS APPROACH AND LIKE WALKED WITH YOUR FRIEND WHILE DISCUSSING CERTAIN THINGS BUT SUDDENLY FELT HEAVY BLOW OF PUNCH ON LOWER STOMACH

REGION,

SPARK WITHOUT FIRE

TOUR FROM INFINITY FOR A REASON

IN FLUCTUATE SEASON

WITH THE HELP OF AVIATION

TO CREATE A NEW VISION

AS AN AUTHOR EYE SLIGHTLY AGREED WITH THE WORDS WHICH SHARED BETWEEN ZERO AND EX BECAUSE EYE QUITE AWARE OF THIS UNCONSCIOUS WALK BUT EYE FOUND SOME UNNTAURAL THINGS WHILE NARRATING THE ZERO HAS ONE STORY , NOW EYE AM WRITING ON A PLATFORM WHICH CALLED SAME 0 & 1 BINARY CODE EXHIBITION AND NOW EVERY SPECIES FEELS THE SAME AS EYE HAVE A FEELING ABOUT THIS 0 & 1 BINARY TOUR THAT EYE AM AT THE TOP OF WORLD IN THIS ERA OF DIGITALIZATION ,

AS AN AUTHOR EYE ALWAYS FELT ANNOYED BECAUSE BEFORE IF EYE OYSTERED FOR ANY EVEN SMALL INFORMATION I HAD TO WAIT FOR A LONG TIME BUT NOW IF EYE PANTING FOR ANY INFORMATION ITS SOMETHING LIKE THE WORLD IS IN MY OYSTER

FOR LIFE INVIGORATION, BUT EYE HAD TO ACCEPT THAT FACT ABOUT JOURNEY OF ZERO, WAS NOT THAT EASY AS NOW WHICH EYE ADVOCATING THE 0 & 1 BINARY ARTIFICIAL INTELLIGENCE FOR EVERY WEB WEDDING WORK STATION ,

NOW ALL SPECIES ARE LIVING UPTO HIGHEST MARK BECAUSE OF HIGH LEVEL OF ARTIFICIAL INTELLIGENCE TECHNOLOGY INNOVATION BUT AS AN AUTHOR WHEN EYE LEAF THROUGH THE STORY OF ZERO FOR THE ONE IN A TRIANGLE ROUTE WHICH GUIDED BY THE EX THEN EYE REALISED THAT MANY MORE THINGS TO RE DISCOVER WHICH HAS BEEN BURRIED WITH NOISES IN THIS TRIANGLE ROUTE OF EXHUMATION ,

SPARK WITHOUT FIRE

TOUR FROM INFINITY FOR REASON

IN FLUCTUATE SEASON

WITH THE HELP OF AVIATION

TO CREATE A NEW VISION

ZERO WAS HANGING ON TO THE WORDS OF EX AND PROMISED EX THAT WOULD READY TO BRAZEN OUT ANY KIND OF DIFFICULTIES AS WELL AS STORMS IN THIS TRINAGLE ROUTE OF CONSCIOUS AND UNCONSCIOUS ARTICULATION ,

TRIANGLE ROUTE IN DARKNESS OF CIRCLE

EX TOLD ZERO ABOUT ALL THE MEDIUMS OF LIGHT .SOUND , CRYSTALL CLEAR GLASSES WHERE THEY PROBABLY WOULD GET COUPLE OF PROSPECTIVE RESULTS WHILE TRAVERSE THROUGH THESE TRIANGLE ROUTE MEDIUM AND THE FIRST PROSPECTIVE RESULT MAY BE DISSAPPOINT YOU ZERO BUT THIS IS FACT AND WOULD BE CHANCE OF VANISH OR DISAPPEAR AT ANY PART OF THIS ROUTE AND THE SECOND ONE MIGHT BE REACHED THE DESTINATION BUT CAN'T ASSURE THAT ONE TO WHOM YOU ARE LOOK FOR RECOGNIZATION ,

SPARK WITHOUT FIRE

TOUR FROM INFINITY FOR A REASON

IN FLUCTUATE SEASON

WITH THE HELP OF AVIATION

TO CREATE A NEW VISION

AS AS NON -NATIVE SPEAKER AND AN AUTHOR OF " SPARK WITHOUT FIRE" EVEN EYE STARTED ANALYSIS ON THIS PHRASES LIKE MIGHT BE FEEL COMPLETE DISAPPEAR OR MIGHT BE DISSAPPOINTMENT IF WON'T GET THE REAL ONE OF JUBILATION , NOW WHAT HAPPENED ,AS AN USER I HAVE BEEN EXPERIENCING MANY ERROR LIKE THE THINGS WHICH EYE CAN'T EXPECT THESE KIND OF WORDS IN THIS LARGER THAN LIFE ARTIFICIAL INTELLIGENCE AND IT WON'T ACCEPTABLE FOR NATURAL FUTURISTIC DEPICTION ,

AFTER DEEP ANALYSIS ON ZERO 'S ONE TRIANGLE ROUTE WORDS , EYE REALIZED ONE THING THAT SOMETHING WENT WRONG IN THIS CRAZY DIGITALIZATION BECAUSE AS A WEB USER WHEN EYE HAVE BEEN ENCOUNTERD WITH THE SAME

QUESTION WHILE WEB BROWSING THAT ARE YOU ROBOT ? ON EVERY WEB PAGES , THEN IT MEANS A LOT FOR ME AND THIS IS SOMETHING OUT OF SOMETHING, PERHAPS HAVE TO HIRED SOME ONE TO GET RID OF SUCH WEB ISSUES AND MADE ME FREE FROM THIS ANSWER NO .EYE AM NOT ROBOT OF THIS RIDICULE QUESTION ,

EYE BELIEVE THIS WON'T BE A SMALL ISSUE BECAUSE EYE NEVER HEARD THAT ROBOT MEANS THE MACHINE HAS STARTED ASKING USER THAT ARE YOU A ROBOT ? SOMETIMES AS A WEB USER EYE THOUGHT HOW EYE REACT TO THIS ROBOT'S QUESTION BECAUSE EYE DON'T KNOW IF EYE SAY YES TO THE ROBOT'S QUESTION THEN WHAT WOULD BE THE NEXT QUESTION FOR ME FROM THE ROBOT AND SOMETIMES EYE CONFUSED THAT WHICH ERA EYE AM RESIDING RIGHT NOW FOR LIFE RESUSCITATION

..

Spark Without Fire

TOUR FROM INFINITY FOR A REASON
IN FLUCTUATE SEASON
WITH THE HELP OF AVIATION
TO CREATE A NEW VISION

WITH THE MINUTES OF DISCUSSION WITH EX FINALLY ZERO WAS REALIZED ABOUT THE LIGHT BECAUSE THIS WAS THE MEDIUM OF EXCELLENCE WHICH WOULD HELP ZERO TO FIND OUT THE ONE , BUT THE LIGHT ROUTE WAS NOT EASY AS WELL AS NOT ACCESSIBLE FOR EVERY ONE ,ONE CAN UNDERSTAND THE SOUND ROUTE BUT THE LIGHT JOURNEY THROUGH THE TRIANGLE ,IT SEEMS SOUND LIKE A KIND OF REFRACTION ,

ZERO WAS NEVER EXPERIENCING SUCH KIND OF TOUR AND WITH LIGHT ZERO HAD TO BE MORE CONSCIOUS BECAUSE WHEN LIGHTS TRAVERSE THROUGH TRIANGLE ROUTE ,IT CONSTANTLY CHANGING ITS SPEED WHILE CROSSING THE BORDERS , NOW ZERO HAD FIX ONE THING IN ITS FEEBLE MIND THAT THE LIGHT IS THE ONLY WITNESS OF ALL TIMES LIKE PAST ,PRESENT AND FUTURE DUE TO THIS CHANGING OF SPEED OF LIGHT IN DIRECTION ,

ZERO WAS TRIED TO AVOID ALL KIND OF ERRORS ON THE WAY OF THIS ONE INCLINATION BECAUSE ZERO DIDN'T KNOW BEFORE THAT THINGS WHICH LOOKS AND SOUNDS EASY ,IN FACT IT WAS NOT EASY IN THIS LOOPHOLE OF TRIANGLE VERSION.

THE STORY TO BECONTINUED IN CHAPTER -3

Spark Without Fire

TOUR FROM INFINTY FOR A REASON
IN FLUCTUATE SEASON
WITH THE HELP OF AVIATION
TO CREATE A NEW VISION

AS AN AUTHOR EYE FIGURED OUT THIS WAS A NEVER ENDING CHAPTERS OF ZERO AND WHEN EYE LEAF THROUGH THE MEDIUMS THEN ENVISAGE OF COUPLE OF THINGS HAPPENED WITH ZERO EITHER FIND THE RIGHT ONE FOR THE HEALTHY CONSTRUCTION OR THESE LIGHT CARDS SAYS A POSSIBLE DESTRUCTION IN THIS TRIANGLE ROUTE OF AN INNER DARK CIRCLE, AS A TRAVEL PROFESSIONAL ALSO EYE HAVE BEEN THROUGH MANY DIFFERENT TIME ZONES OF LIGHT AND FERRETED OUT MANY DARK STORIES WHICH HAS CREATED BY LIGHT IN ITS MOTION

TO BE COTINUED IN CHAPTER - 3

Spark Without Fire

AS AN AUTHOR EYE HAVE BEEN TRYING TO AVOID SPELLING MISTAKES IN MY WRITING FOR MANY YEARS ,IF FOUND SOME MISTAKES IN WORDS SPELLING THEN PLEASE DONOT MISS-TAKE ME .

EYE DON'T HAVE CAPTION FOR SPARK WITHOUT FIRE

GYAN CHAND PATTANAYAK WITH PRABHAT MANJARI PATTNAYAK

AUTHOR INFORMATION -:

GYAN CHAND PATTANAYAK

MOBILE NO- +91 7853045594

+91 7681830729

Printed by Libri Plureos GmbH in Hamburg,
Germany